Inspir

Nautical Poems

and

Prose

—to keep you on your toes

James Scott Bernard

Copyright © 2015
By
James Scott Bernard
—
Bernard Publishing
Warrenton, Oregon 97146
ISBN 978-0-9961665-2-2

James Scott Bernard

Dedication

This simple work is dedicated to all seafarers and those who love the sea—those living and those who have given their lives to the sea.

Better words than those expressed in Psalm 107 cannot be formed to describe the lives of "those who go down to the sea in ships."

Psalm 107

Those who go down to the sea in ships, who do business in great waters, they see the works of the Lord, and His wonders in the deep. For He commands and raises the stormy wind, which lifts up the waves of the sea.

They mount up to the Heavens. They go down again to the depths; their soul melts because of trouble. They reel to and fro, and stagger like a drunken man; and are at their wits' end.

Then they cry out to the Lord in their trouble. And He brings them out of their distresses. He calms the storm, so that waves are still. Then they are glad because they are quiet. So He guides them to their desired Heaven.

Contents

2	Columbia River Bar
4	It Came to Pass
6	Wake of Life
8	Chart Your Course
10	Get Out of the Comfort Zone
12	Sail Your Ship
14	Gimbals of Grace
16	Dreaming or Steaming?
18	Persistence
20	Life Storms
22	Getting On with Our Lives
24	'Tis the Bold That Get the Gold
26	Something to Hold On to
28	Faith
30	Collision Course
32	Aloha
34	Butterfly Watch
36	He Never Tried
38	Keeps Us Fishing
40	A Little Patch of Beauty
42	Always There for Me
44	The Fog Lifted
46	Uncharted Waters

Psalm 107:23

Those who go down to the sea in ships, who do business on great waters ...

The Columbia River Bar

I'm heading for the Columbia River Bar.
I've been there many times before.
But friend, it'll never be a bore.
One minute calm, the next it's war.

I'm heading for the Columbia River Bar.
I've been there many times before.
The buoy's moan, the frothing foam,
Make ya wonder why you roam.

I'm heading for the Columbia River Bar.
I've been there many times before.
If the sea could talk, we'd probably get out and walk.
For the tales that could be told, of the
Frightened and the bold, of ships laden with gold
How far beneath the cold.

I'm heading for the Columbia River Bar.
I've been there many times before.
With the South Jetty on my stern,
I know some day I'll return—I'll be heading
For the Columbia River Bar.
I've been there many times before.

Galatians 6:1

Brethern, if a man is overtaken in any trespass, you who are spiritual restore such a one in a spirit of gentleness ...

Hold Course

In navigation the "Rules of the Road" calls for the vessel being over taken by another to hold course until the overtaking vessel has passed.

It seems to me the same is true in life when we're being "over taken" by trials, temptation or tribulation: "Hold Course!" And remember, "It Came to Pass,"

It Came to Pass

O' Lord this problem or pain
How long will it last?
Just remember, "It will come to pass"
I'm so tired and weary,
Will I be able to last?
O' Lord I don't feel I'm able to tackle this task
Just remember, "It will come to pass"
When faced with the trails and
temptations of life
Just remember it came to pass.

Thessalonians 3:9

But to make ourselves an example of how you should follow us.

Wake of Life

On a beautiful sunny morning in Alaska, I watched a float plane take off from Yes Bay. The water was as smooth as glass.

As the plane took off, it made quite a wake. Long after the plane had disappeared in the distance, the wake of the plane continued to lap upon the shore.

I thought how similar this is to our existence. The "unique wake" of our being will continue to lap upon the shores of those remaining long after we have disappeared in the distance.

ଛଠ

Psalm 90:12

So teach us to number our days that we might apply our hearts unto wisdom.

Chart Your Course

O' Friend chart your course, and capture the force that will make your journey full of purpose and joy.

For the time that is ours may be like the flowers, blooming today and tomorrow withering away. Set goals that will challenge the best that's within—pulling us forward, helping us win.

O' Friend chart your course, for the greatest remorse is to leave this course—never knowing how great was your force!

Romans 12:2

Be not conformed to this world but be transformed by the renewal of your mind ...

Getting Out of the Comfort Zone

Force yourself into a little adventure. Learn something new. I just talked with a man who started to ski at eighty-six. David Clark at seventy-seven circumnavigated the globe and said, "I wanted to send a message that dreams are achievable."

Jesus said: "Cast your nets on the other side:" i.e. do something different. Put some fresh air into your life before it becomes stale.

Psalm 90:12

So teach us to number our days that we might apply our hearts unto wisdom.

Sail Your Ship

O' friend said your ship
Climb your mountain
Life passes so fast
Make the most of it while it lasts.

Ford those streams
Fulfill your dreams
Life passes so fast
Make the most of it while it lasts.

While it lasts,
Be filled with the love
That comes from above
Share it with others
We're all sisters and brothers.
Live passes so fast
Make the most of it while it lasts.

Philippians 4:12

I know how to be abased and I know how to abound ...

Gimbals of Grace

The ships compass is mounted in "Gimbals" so that no matter what the "pitch" or "roll" of the ship, the compass remains level.

I believe it's by the "Grace of God" we're given "Human Gimbals" enabling us to keep a level head no matter what the pitch or roll of life brings us.

౸౸

James 2:20

Faith without works is dead.

Dreaming or Steaming

Are you drifting and dreaming when you should be steering and steaming? Are you waiting and resting when you should be investing the potential within to gain a real win.

>Steaming stead of Dreaming
>Investing stead of Resting
>Then they'll be no Guessing
>You'll receive a "Big Blessing."

I Corinthians 9:24

Do you not know that those who run in a race all run, but only one receives the prize? Run in such a way that you may win.

Persistence

On a trip to the Oregon Coast clam digging, I was experiencing very poor results. I would spot the small oval in the sand where I was certain there would be a clam, dig with great "fury," but no clam. Finally, I thought maybe I'm not digging deep enough. Sure enough, by digging just a few inches deeper—Bingo! A clam every time! Important point: It takes almost as much effort to almost get a clam as it does to get one. It takes almost as much effort to almost succeed as it does to succeed.

Matthew 8:24-27

And suddenly a great tempest arose on the sea, so that the boat was covered with the waves, but He was asleep. His disciples came to Him and awoke Him saying, "Lord save us!" He said to them, "Why are you fearful, you of little faith?" Then he arose and rebuked the wind and sea—and there was a great calm.

Life Storms

O' Lord my life is like a stormy sea,
Which way shall I go, where shall I flee?
The waves of despair seem to be everywhere.
My courage and pride has ebbed like the tide.
O' Calm the winds of my doubt and
Bring me about.
Make change in me so at peace I will be
And a Blessing to Thee"

Philippians 3:13

Forgetting those things which are behind and reaching forward to those things which are ahead.

Getting On with Our Lives

On several occasions, while drift fishing on Oregon streams, our boat would slip into an "eddy" out of the main stream and unless extra effort in rowing took place, the boat would remain trapped in the eddy, the "circular" motion of the water.

Many of our lives get trapped in an "eddy" of circumstances or habit that keeps us from moving on in the main stream of life. We need to take the Oars of Thought and Action, redefining our short and long term goals and move on into the main stream of our futures.

Proverbs 28:1

But the righteous are bold as a lion.

'Tis the Bold that Get the Gold

Aye Maties, 'tis the bold that get the gold.
If ya sit back and wait you'll be left
Hanging at the gate.
For 'tis the bold that get the gold.
If you never take a chance it's a cinch
You won't advance.
For 'tis the bold that get the gold.
'Tis true opportunity all around us knocks.
But it's up to us to break the mental locks.
For 'tis the bold that get the gold.
Many tales have been told about a man's
Elusive search for gold,
But they'll all be losers in the cold,
Until they grasp the truth—
'Tis the bold that get the Gold!

Psalm 31:3

For you are my rock and fortress.

Psalm 46:1

A very present help in time of need.

Something to Hold On to

Many years ago before the days of seat belts, I was driving my young son to a Cub Scout meeting. All of a sudden the car in front of us made an abrupt stop.

I hollered, "Hang on!" My young son's response was, "But Dad there's nothing to hang on to!"

How many of us in times of crisis find ourselves looking for something to "hang on to."

We need to find an "anchor" a "rock" for our lives, something to hang on to" before the crisis arrives: what is yours?

Hebrews 11:1

Now faith is the substance of things hoped for, the evidence of things not seen.

Faith

What is faith? It's occupying new territory. It's seeking new horizons. It's stretching and reaching beyond familiar ground.

Faith is for the upward and outward bound. It is not seeing, it is just believing there's a better way, causing and influencing our every sway.

What is faith? It's acting on ideas, excepting the best, not giving up when we're put to the test. It's putting our life on the line, going for broke each and every time. For faith is the force that makes victory our course.

What is faith? It's occupying new territory. It's seeking new horizons. It's stretching and reaching beyond familiar ground. Faith is for the upward and outward bound.

Galatians 6:7

Do not be deceived. God is not mocked; for whatever a man sows, that he will also reap.

Collision Course

In navigation when your ship sights an approaching vessel and the bearing of the other vessel doesn't change, it indicates that you are on a "collision course' and unless you change course you will collide with the other vessel.

Life is kind of that way. If we keep following the same "life" course that's producing negative result we'll keep colliding with bad results. If we want positive results we must change course.

You're at the helm, the captain of your ship and you decide which way your life will go.

James 1:22

But be doers of the word and not hearers only.

Aloha

Aloha. Aloha! What a strange word.

It means hello, and it means goodbye. Whether you're heading out or returning, via sea or by sky, why not say aloha, goodbye, to ways that lead nowhere, and say aloha, hello, to ways that lead somewhere.

Say aloha, goodbye, to that which is less than your best. Say aloha, hello, to that which puts pride in your chest. Say aloha, goodbye, to hate and to fear; say aloha, hello, to love and good cheer.

Say aloha, hello, to all that's positive in life. Say aloha, goodbye, to all negation and strife. Aloha, aloha, what a strange word. It means hello and it means goodbye.

Colossians 3:15

And let the peace of God rule in your hearts.

The Butterfly Watch

I was crossing the Pacific on a voyage from Korea to Portland, Oregon aboard a Liberty ship when we encountered heavy seas and the ships propeller would come out of the water as we came off a heavy sea. Unless the ship's engines' RPMs were immediately reduced the ship would shake violently causing possible damage to the ship. This was referred to as a "Butterfly Watch."

It seems to me the same is true in our lives, when faced with the "heavy seas" of life, be it trials of human relationships, financial problems, health or just a hopeless feeling. Rather than let it cause harm to you, go on the "Butterfly Watch;" slow down, pray up, take the pressure off yourself, relax and like the ship and you'll reach home port in good shape.

Matthew 25:25

And I was afraid, and went and hid your talent.

He Never Tried

He could have been a ship builder,
Almost any profession was within his stride,
But he never tired.

He could have scaled the mountains high,
Or sailed the whole world wide,
But he never tired.

Some say it was because of or the lack of pride,
But he never tired.

Great songs unsung, so many things undone,
Remain inside,
Because he never tired.
The joys that were missed, the friends eclipsed,
Because he never tired.

When opportunity has passed, and he's about to breath his last, he broke down and bitterly cried,
Because he'd never really tired.

I Corinthians 2:9

Eye has not seen, nor ear heard, nor have entered into the heart of man the things which God has prepared for those who love Him.

Keeps Us Fishing

Sometimes we tend to think that "knowing" is the key to "peace of mind" or "happiness." But if we knew exactly what was going to happen, how things were going to be, the "dynamism" of life would be missing.

It's not knowing that puts "zip" into life. Each day is brand new, a never been lived before day. Who knows what adventure awaits us?

That's why "not knowing" keeps us fishing, going to sporting events and getting up each morning.

Thank you Lord for not letting us know!

Philippians 4:8

Finally, brethren whatever things are true, whatever things are noble, whatever things are just, whatever things are pure, whatever things are lovely, whatever things are good report; if there is any virtue and if there is anything praiseworthy—meditate on these things.

A Little Patch of Beauty

While jogging one morning, I passed a small, old run-down home which appeared as though it had barely survived many a coastal storm. But in stark contrast to the rest of the surrounding was a small three-foot by three-foot patch of beauty where the residents had planted beautiful tulips which were in full bloom.

I thought how the old home was similar to many of our lives—often battered by the trials, sorrows and disappointments in life. But yet if we keep at least a little patch of beauty, be it pleasant memories of the past, at least a mustard seed of faith or all the positive things we have left, and focus on these, our own little Patch of Beauty, life will remain good and we'll be given the strength to go on.

Matthew 28:20

Lo I am with you always.

Psalm 139:9

If I take the wings of the morning and dwell in the uttermost parts of the sea, even there your hand shall lead me, and your right hand shall hold me.

Always There for Me

Lord you've always been there for me,
Whether on the mountain tops
Or in the desperate depths of the sea.

Lord you've always been there for me,
In sickness or health,
Poverty or wealth.

Lord you've always been there for me,
In times of doubt and fear
You've been especially near.

Lord you've always been there for me,
Thank you Lord and praise your name!
You've always been there for me.

ಐಒ

I Peter 2:9

Proclaim the praises of Him who called you out of darkness into His marvelous light.

The Fog Lifted

On a recent early morning in Alaska, as I looked out my window I saw the bay covered with dense fog. As the morning progressed, I could see the sun slowly breaking through. Sure enough little-by-little the warmth and light of the sun burned off all the fog exposing a beautiful clear day.

I got to thinking how many of our lives seem to get lost in a fog of doubt, despair, uncertainty and hopelessness. Yet, if we seek and let the light of truth in and we continue to nourish with warmth our little seed of faith, the way becomes clearer. Hope returns and doubts disappear and just like a beautiful clear day, life becomes beautiful again.

ಶುಭ

I Peter 2:9

Who called you out of darkness into His marvelous light ...

Isaiah 43:16

Thus says the Lord, who makes a way in the sea and a path through mighty waters ...

Uncharted Waters

I guess most of us find ourselves in "Uncharted Waters" at one point of another in our lives.

O' we start our lives in familiar waters, many ports of call on the Horizon—friendly seas and tropical breeze. We make our voyage with great ease, then the storms of life come upon us and we find ourselves in "Uncharted Waters." What do we say when we find ourselves in "Uncharted Waters?"

Do you say: "I can't survive, I'll surely die? O' why O' why did this have to happen to me?

When the storms of life come upon you and you find yourself in "Uncharted Waters." What can you do? You look to your "Master Pilot" when you are in "Uncharted Waters." He will guide you through all troubled waters.

Yes He will guide you through all "Uncharted Waters."

About the Author

At the age of sixteen Jim Bernard crossed the Columbia River Bar as an ordinary seaman. He received his Deck Officer's license at twenty-one and served during the Korean War.

In college, Jim majored in business, psychology, and religion.

Jim was the CEO and principle owner of a real estate and insurance company for thirty years in the Portland Area. After selling the business, he and his wife Cherie moved to the Astoria area where Jim assisted in the management of a Ford dealership until recently.

Jim presently serves as a captain and guide in Alaska during the summer months.

Also by the Author

Positive Poems and Rhymes to Encourage Your Times

Positive Thoughts for a Profitable Day

Making the Principles of Success a Habit

Alaska Fishing Adventures (2015)

Contact

For comment or additional information, Jim Bernard can be reached at:

JamesBernard711@aol.com

503-680-2366

James Scott Bernard
Author/Publisher
870 NW Fir Avenue
Warrenton, Oregon 97146
USA

Made in the USA
Charleston, SC
18 June 2015